Great National Soccer Teams / Grandes selecciones del fútbol mundial

ENGLAND / INGLATERRA

José María Obregón

English translation: Megan Benson

PowerKiDS press™

Editorial Buenas Letras™
New York

Published in 2010 by The Rosen Publishing Group, Inc.
29 East 21st Street, New York, NY 10010

First Edition

Editor: Nicole Pristash
Book Design: Julio Gil
Photo Researcher: Jessica Gerweck

Photo Credits: Cover Laurence Griffiths/Getty Images; back cover, p. 19 Bob Thomas/Getty Images; p. 5 Phil Cole/Getty Images; pp. 7, 13 Hulton Archive/Getty Images; p. 9 Central Press/Getty Images; p. 11 Bentley Archive/Popperfoto/Getty Images; p. 15 Clive Rose/Getty Images; p. 17 Martin Rose/Bongarts/Getty Images; p. 21 (flag) Shutterstock.com; p. 21 (left) Ben Radford/Allsport/Getty Images; p. 21 (middle) Douglas Miller/Keystone/Getty Images; p. 21 Christof Koepsel/Bongarts/Getty Images.

Library of Congress Cataloging-in-Publication Data

Obregón, José María, 1963–
   England = Inglaterra / José María Obregón. — 1st ed.
      p. cm. — (Great national soccer teams = Grandes selecciones nacionales de fútbol)
   Includes index.
   ISBN 978-1-4042-8089-2 (library binding) — ISBN 978-1-4358-3235-0 (pbk.) —
ISBN 978-1-4358-3236-7 (6-pack)
   1. Soccer—England—Juvenile literature. 2. Soccer teams—England—Juvenile literature. I. Title.
II. Title: Inglaterra.
   GV944.G7O27 2010
   796.3340942—dc22
                                        2009000777

Manufactured in the United States of America

CONTENTS

CONTENIDO

The British national soccer team is a great team. England is one of the seven countries that have won the **World Cup**. English players Gordon Banks, Bobby Charlton, Paul Gascoigne, and Michael Owen are among the best soccer players in the world.

La selección de fútbol de Inglaterra es un gran equipo. Inglaterra es uno de los siete países que han ganado la **Copa del Mundo**. Además, jugadores ingleses como Gordon Banks, Bobby Charlton, Paul Gascoine y Michael Owen se encuentran entre los mejores jugadores del mundo.

British players celebrated after John Terry (center, number 6) scored a goal in 2008.

El jugador inglés John Terry (al centro, número 6) celebra tras anotar un gol en 2008.

Soccer has been played around the world for many centuries. Rule-based soccer games were first played in British high schools in the mid-1800s. The teachers at the schools made the rules up themselves. Some of those rules are still a part of the game today.

El fútbol se ha jugado en todo el mundo durante siglos. Cuando el fútbol llegó a las escuelas de Inglaterra, en el siglo 17, los profesores comenzaron a escribir las reglas de lo que sería el fútbol moderno. Muchas de estas reglas continúan en la actualidad.

This drawing from 1891 shows a match between British teams, the Blackburn Rovers and Notts County.

Este dibujo de 1891 muestra un partido entre los equipos Blackburn Rovers y Notts County.

7

Along with Scotland's, England's soccer team is the oldest national team in the world. England and Scotland played the first **international** soccer match in history. The game took place on November 30, 1872, in Partick, Scotland. The game ended in a tie.

Junto con Escocia, la selección de Inglaterra es la selección más antigua del mundo. Inglaterra y Escocia jugaron en el primer partido **internacional** de fútbol de la historia. El partido fue el 30 de noviembre de 1872, en Partick, Escocia. El partido terminó con un empate.

This picture shows the leaders of old rivals Scotland (left) and England (right) before a game in 1957.

Aquí vemos a los grandes rivales, Escocia (izquierda) e Inglaterra (derecha) antes de un partido en 1957.

9

England won its first World Cup in 1966. The **tournament** was played in England. The British team beat Germany in an exciting final match. The game was decided in overtime, or extra time added to the end of a game. England won, 4–2. British player Geoff Hurst scored three goals!

Inglaterra ganó su primera Copa del Mundo en 1966. El **torneo** se llevó a cabo en Inglaterra, y los ingleses vencieron a Alemania en un emocionante partido que acabó en tiempo extra. Inglaterra ganó 4 a 2. ¡El jugador inglés Geoff Hurst anotó tres goles en el partido final!

Here British player Geoff Hurst (right) is shown scoring a goal during the 1966 World Cup final.

El jugador inglés Geoff Hurst (derecha) anota un gol durante la final de la Copa del Mundo 1966.

ENGLAND 3 GERMANY W. 2

11

One of England's great players from the past is Bobby Moore. Moore played 108 games with England. In 1966, he was the captain of the national team that won the World Cup. In 1964, Moore was named the best player in England.

Bobby Moore es considerado el mejor jugador inglés de la historia. Moore jugó 108 partidos con la selección de Inglaterra y fue capitán del equipo campeón del mundo en 1966. En 1963, Moore fue nombrado el mejor jugador de Inglaterra.

Bobby Moore kisses the trophy after winning the World Cup final in 1966.

Bobby Moore besa el trofeo tras ganar la final de la Copa del Mundo 1966.

13

England's national team is known for its **tough**, fast players. British players have a very quick playing style. They move the ball with great speed. In just a moment, British players can go from keeping the ball out of their net to scoring a goal!

El estilo de juego de la selección de Inglaterra se basa en la **fuerza** y la velocidad de sus jugadores. La selección de Inglaterra mueve el balón con mucha velocidad. ¡En un momento pueden pasar de la defensa al ataque y anotar un gol!

Wayne Rooney, shown here, plays with the speed and strength for which British players are known.

Wayne Rooney muestra la velocidad y la fuerza que distingue a los jugadores ingleses.

David Beckham is the most famous member of England's national team. Beckham plays the midfielder position. As a midfielder, Beckham's job is to get the ball, pass it, and sometimes score. Beckham is the only British player who has scored goals in three World Cups.

David Beckham es el jugador inglés más famoso de los últimos años. Beckham juega en la posición de medio volante. Como medio volante, su trabajo es pasar el balón, y en ocasiones, anotar goles. Beckham es el único jugador inglés que ha anotado en tres Copas del Mundo.

David Beckham (right) is shown here controlling the ball during a game against Switzerland in 2004.

David Beckham (derecha) controla el balón durante un partido contra Suiza en 2004.

England has always been a powerful team in Europe. However, England has never won the European Football Championship, which is the most important tournament in Europe. The farthest the team reached in the tournament was the semifinal game in 1996.

Inglaterra siempre ha sido una selección muy poderosa en Europa. Sin embargo, los ingleses nunca han podido ganar la EUROCOPA, el torneo más importante del continente. Su mejor resultado fue en 1996, cuando avanzaron hasta la semifinal del torneo.

Here England is shown playing in Wembley Stadium during the 1996 European Football Championship.

El equipo de Inglaterra en el estadio de Wembley, en Londres, durante la EUROCOPA 1996.

19

England is working hard, though, to win its second World Cup and to become European champions for the first time. Young players, such as Wayne Rooney, Theo Walcott, and Gabriel Agbonlahor, are helping the team remain one of the best national soccer teams in the world.

Inglaterra trabaja muy fuerte para ganar su segunda Copa del Mundo y convertirse en campeones de Europa por primera ocasión. Hoy, las jóvenes estrellas inglesas como Wayne Rooney, Theo Walcott y Gabriel Agbonlahor ayudan a que Inglaterra siga siendo una de las mejores selecciones del mundo.

ENGLAND  INGLATERRA

The Football Association Ltd.
Year Founded: 1863

Asociación de Fútbol Ltd.
Año de Fundación: 1863

 Home / Local

 Away / Visitante

Player Highlights / Jugadores destacados

Most Caps* / Más convocatorias

Peter Shilton (1970–1990)
125 caps / 125 convocatorias

* Appearances with the national soccer team

Top Scorer / Mejor anotador

Sir Robert "Bobby" Charlton
(1958–1970)
49 goals / 49 goles

Most Famous Player / Jugador más famoso

David Beckham (1996–)
Only English player to score in three
World Cups / Único jugador inglés
que ha anotado en 3 Copas
del Mundo

Team Highlights / Palmarés del equipo

FIFA World Cup™ / Copa Mundial FIFA
  Appearances / Participaciones: 12
  Winner / Ganador: 1966
  Fourth / Cuarto: 1990

UEFA European Football Championship /
EUROCOPA UEFA
  Semifinalist / Semifinalista: 1996

FIFA U-20 World Cup / Copa Mundial FIFA Sub-20
  Fourth / Cuarto: 1981

GLOSSARY / GLOSARIO

international (in-tur-NA-shuh-nul) Having to do with more than one country.

tough (TUF) Strong or firm.

tournament (TOR-nuh-ment) A group of games that decides the best team.

World Cup (WUR-uld KUP) A tournament that takes place every four years with teams from around the world.

Copa del Mundo (la) Competencia de fútbol, cada 4 años, en la que juegan los mejores equipos del mundo.

fuerza (la) Con energía, con ánimo.

internacional Que tiene que ver con más de un país.

torneo (el) Un grupo de partidos que deciden cuál es el mejor equipo.

RESOURCES / RECURSOS

Books in English / Libros en inglés

Gifford, Clive. *The Kingfisher Soccer Encyclopedia*. Boston: Houghton Mifflin Harcourt, 2006.

Savage, Jeff. *David Beckham*. Minneapolis: First Avenue Editions, 2008.

Books in Spanish / Libros en español

Dann, Sarah. *Fútbol en acción (Soccer in Action)*. New York: Crabtree Publishing, 2005.

Obregón, José María. *David Beckham*. New York: PowerKids Press/Editorial Buenas Letras, 2008.

Web Sites

Due to the changing nature of Internet links, PowerKids Press has developed an online list of Web sites related to the subject of this book. This site is updated regularly. Please use this link to access the list:
www.powerkidslinks.com/soct/england/

INDEX

ÍNDICE